EXTREME
SPORTS AND STUNTS™

EXTREME
NINJA WARRIOR

Carla Mooney

rosen publishing's
rosen central®

New York

Published in 2020 by The Rosen Publishing Group, Inc.
29 East 21st Street, New York, NY 10010

Cataloging-in-Publication Data

Names: Mooney, Carla, author.
Title: Extreme ninja warrior / Carla Mooney.
Description: First edition. | New York : Rosen Publishing, 2020. | Series: Extreme sports
and stunts | Audience: Grades 5–8. | Includes bibliographical references and index.
Identifiers: ISBN 9781725347403 (library bound) | ISBN 9781725347397 (paperback)
Subjects: LCSH: Obstacle racing—Juvenile literature. | Obstacle racing—
Training—Juvenile literature. | Extreme sports—Juvenile literature.
Classification: LCC GV1067.M66 2020 | DDC 796.42'6—dc23

Manufactured in the United States of America

Disclaimer: Do not attempt this sport without wearing proper
safety gear and taking safety precautions.

CONTENTS

INTRODUCTION

In September 2015, some of the best ninja warrior athletes in the country gathered in Las Vegas, Nevada, for the *American Ninja Warrior* National Finals. The finals course is a daunting four-stage beast in which athletes face one challenging obstacle after another. Each athlete gets a single chance to complete a stage. One mistake and the athlete is out of the competition. In 2015, thirty-eight athletes finished the first stage. Eight completed the second stage. By the end of the third stage, only two competitors were left standing: Geoff Britten and Isaac Caldiero.

The two men were the first competitors in history to attempt the final stage of the competition. The challenge in front of them: climb a tower using a 75-foot (23 meter) rope. As an added twist, competitors had to make the climb in thirty seconds or less. Britten went first. He used his strong arms to power his way up the rope and hit the buzzer at the top of the tower with 0.35 seconds to spare. He was the first athlete to complete the American Ninja Warrior finals course.

Britten's victory would be short-lived. Caldiero grabbed the rope and began to climb for his shot at Total Victory and the competition's $1 million prize. Caldiero's long history of rock climbing gave him the strength to propel himself up the tower. He reached the top and hit the buzzer with 3.86 seconds left. With his faster time, Caldiero became the first and only winner—as of 2018—of *American Ninja Warrior*.

Ninja warrior Isaac Caldiero leaps from one part of the Flying Squirrel obstacle to the next while competing at a qualifying event for the Ultimate Ninja Athlete Association.

Some of the toughest athletes in the world battle through unpredictable obstacles and grueling courses in extreme ninja warrior competitions. Millions of fans watch every run on the course. They cheer as competitors make it through each obstacle and groan when they fail. While the television competition show *American Ninja Warrior* has made the extreme sport mainstream, everyday people can train and compete in ninja warrior gyms and local competitions. For fans and athletes alike, extreme ninja warrior competitions have become one of the most thrilling sports today.

CHAPTER ONE

THE WORLD'S MOST DEMANDING OBSTACLE COURSE

In the middle of the night, a rookie competitor bounces on his feet and stretches his arms at the beginning of the *American Ninja Warrior* course. He landed his spot in the competition as a walk-on, one of about 100 athletes chosen by the show's producers to compete this night. He takes a deep breath and waves to his family in the audience. The clock starts and he leaps onto one of the world's toughest obstacle courses.

Introduced in the United States in 2009, *American Ninja Warrior* is a hit television show that follows hundreds of athletes as they tackle some of the world's most difficult obstacle courses. Each course consists of a series of obstacles that test an athlete's agility, balance, endurance, upper body strength, and grip strength.

SASUKE: JAPANESE NINJA WARRIOR

American Ninja Warrior is based on Japan's *SASUKE* or Ninja Warrior competition. *SASUKE* debuted in 1997 on Japanese television. It became one of Japan's top sports entertainment shows. The show gathered 100 athletes to compete on a difficult four-stage obstacle course. When American audiences began to show interest in *SASUKE*, a small American television network called the G4 Network decided to try an American version of the obstacle course competition. *American Ninja Warrior* became a smash hit for the small network.

Eventually, the show was picked up by NBC. Today, there are nearly twenty different versions of *SASUKE* worldwide. Ninja Warrior television competition shows are filmed in countries like the United Kingdom, France, Germany, Australia, Hungary, China, and Vietnam. In each competition, athletes compete to master daunting obstacles that test their physical and mental toughness.

CITY QUALIFYING TO NATIONAL FINALS

Inspired by the television shows, athletes across the country compete on ninja warrior city courses. First they must conquer the City Qualifying Round. This course includes six to ten obstacles. Those who finish the City Qualifying Round move on to compete in the City Finals. The City Finals course starts with the same obstacles as the qualifying round but adds more challenges. The top finishers in the City Finals advance to Las Vegas for the National Finals.

In Las Vegas, athletes compete in four stages of Mount Midoriyama, the National Finals course. The finals course is modeled after the famous obstacle course at the Midoriyama outdoor studio in Japan. Ninjas must complete three increasingly difficult stages. Stage One includes eight obstacles that challenge an athlete's speed and agility.

In Stage Two, athletes compete on six obstacles built over water. This part of the course challenges the athletes' strength and endurance. In the first two stages, athletes must finish within a specific time limit. Stage Three features seven or eight obstacles also over water. The obstacles in this stage challenge upper body strength, lower body strength, and leg strength. This is the only stage in the finals with no time limit. Finally, ninjas who complete the first three stages face the final obstacle. In Stage Four, athletes must complete a 75-foot (23 meter) rope climb in less than thirty seconds.

Shown here is a nighttime view of the iconic Warped Wall on the City Finals course in Indianapolis, Indiana, for the television show *American Ninja Warrior* in 2016.

To make the competition even more challenging, ninja athletes have only one chance to complete a course. If they misjudge a jump or their grip slips and they fall, their season may be over. If not enough competitors finish a city course, some athletes who go far and fast may still qualify to go to the National Finals in Las Vegas. However, if a competitor makes a mistake in the National Finals, the athlete is out of the competition.

EVERYDAY NINJAS

Since its debut, thousands of athletes have come forward to compete as ninja warriors. Few are professional athletes. Instead, these men and women are rock climbers, MMA fighters, gymnasts, military members, college students, moms, and dads. Many ninja warriors return season after season and have become fan favorites, such as stuntwoman Jessie Graff or stock trader Kevin Bull. In addition, Ninja warrior competitions are some of the few sporting events where men and women compete on the same course.

In an amateur ninja warrior event in Conyers, Georgia, competitors swing from ring to ring as they attempt to cross a pool of muddy water.

Each season there are rookies that face the ninja warrior obstacles. These newcomers walk to the starting line ready to show their skill and perseverance to get to the end of the course. "You look at these athletes, and they're not your NFL, NBA major league guys," says host Akbar Gbajabiamila in the book *Become an American Ninja Warrior*. "These are ordinary people doing extraordinary things, and they're so relatable to the everyday person."

NINJA GYMS

The popularity of *American Ninja Warrior* has sparked a ninja warrior movement across the United States. Ninja gyms have opened in cities from coast to coast. These gyms give athletes of all ages and skill levels the chance to experience firsthand the challenge of a ninja warrior obstacle course. Many of these gyms offer training

THE ULTIMATE NINJA ATHLETE ASSOCIATION

The Ultimate Ninja Athlete Association (UNAA) is a global organization that organizes a series of ninja obstacle course competitions at gyms around the world. Each year, the UNAA World Series includes many area qualifier competitions, regional competitions, and the Ultimate Ninja World Championship Finals. Each competition in the UNAA World Series is judged based on performance and time. Athletes of all skill levels are able to compete. Top athletes can win cash and prizes.

Ninja warrior athlete Donovan Schneider climbs a Salmon Ladder while training for *American Ninja Warrior* in his barn in Juniata, Nebraska.

programs that develop the body strength, endurance, and skills needed to succeed on a ninja warrior course.

At Ninja Nation in Centennial, Colorado, athletes can find obstacles such as the Floating Steps, the Warped Wall, and the Salmon Ladder. On the Salmon Ladder, athletes challenge themselves by moving a pull-up bar through a series of angled rungs.

At the Obstacle Academy in Edna, Minnesota, coaches train athletes to compete in ninja warrior events. The gym has a youth ninja warrior team that competes in both in-house and national ninja competitions. Team members practice weekly and participate in monthly ninja warrior competitions.

Ninja warriors are extreme athletes. They train hard and push their bodies to the limits. Sometimes they fail and fall on an obstacle. Then, they pick themselves up and get ready to face the next challenging course.

CHAPTER TWO

FROM THE JUMPING SPIDER TO THE WARPED WALL

O ther than a good pair of shoes and athletic wear that lets them move freely, ninja warriors solely rely on their own bodies to make it through the course. Instead of equipment, ninja warriors must conquer the course's infamous obstacles. While some succeed in the test of athlete vs. obstacle, many fail.

Some well-known obstacles first appeared in the original *SASUKE* TV competition, such as the Warped Wall, the Jumping Spider, and the Salmon Ladder. Fans cheer as

A woman attempts to master the Jumping Spider obstacle at a local ninja gym. Ninja gyms across the country offer classes and training for adults and kids.

competitors face these obstacles year after year. Some obstacles come back each year. Others appear only once or come back with changes. Each year, the competition's producers also introduce new obstacles to challenge the athletes.

THE OBSTACLE OF CREATING NEW OBSTACLES

Designing a great obstacle takes a lot of work. On *American Ninja Warrior*, a team of people work together to design and build new obstacles. The ATS Team is a Los Angeles, California–based company that is very involved in creating new obstacles. The ATS Team works with the show's producers to brainstorm ideas for new obstacles.

Ninja warrior Ben Melick displays his strength as he attempts an obstacle for the *American Ninja Warrior* television show in Los Angeles, California.

A great obstacle is the perfect mix of being challenging but not impossible. It is extreme but also safe. It is large but able to be quickly broken down and set up in a new location. Ideas for new obstacles come from just about anywhere—playgrounds, little-known international sports obstacles, fan suggestions, and brainstorming sessions.

Once they have a few ideas, the ATS Team builds a prototype, which is a smaller version of the new obstacles in their warehouse. All obstacles are made at the top-secret ATS facility. Competition organizers like to keep new obstacles hidden so that none of the competitors can get an advantage in training.

NINJA TESTERS

When trying out new obstacles, testers run through the prototype and the team makes adjustments to the obstacle as needed. The team may make the obstacle smaller,

GET A GRIP

Sometimes, the type of grip a ninja uses on an obstacle can mean the difference between reaching the end of the course and dropping off an obstacle into the water. One type of grip is a switch grip, also called a cross grip or an alternating grip. Many ninjas use a switch grip on obstacles where they have to move a free bar like the Salmon Ladder. In a switch grip, the ninja's hands face opposite directions on the bar. A switch grip gives an athlete more stability. This grip can also keep the bar from spinning or rolling away from the ninja's fingers.

steeper, or more or less challenging. "We come back almost every week for testing and retesting before an obstacle is approved," says ANW executive producer Brian Richardson in the book *Become an American Ninja Warrior.* "Then when obstacles are built on the course we test again. We are often tweaking an obstacle right up until we start the competition to make sure it's the right level of difficulty."

American Ninja Warrior has a group of full-time testers for obstacles. Testers are talented athletes themselves. They may be climbers, stunt people, gymnasts, or parkour specialists. Many of the testers are just as good on the course as the ninja competitors. Testers assess each obstacle's safety and difficulty. They look to see how the obstacle affects the body and its muscle groups.

On-location testers run though the course as it is set up for the city competitions. These testers are often local ninja athletes. The competition organizers often run dozens of local testers through a course's obstacle to see how they will react to the course. This type of testing allows the organizers to see how the obstacles work with other obstacles on a course. As testers run the full course, designers adjust

A female athlete jumps over construction pipes in an extreme fitness competition. Fit athletes are often used to test ninja warrior obstacles and courses.

the difficulty of the obstacles by changing angles, holds, and distances.

ICONIC OBSTACLES

One of the most iconic obstacles in ninja warrior competitions is the Warped Wall. The wall is featured on the *American Ninja Warrior* course and is one of the oldest obstacles in *SASUKE* history. The wall has a short runway that leads to a sharply curving wall that soars 14.5 feet (4.4 meters) high. On *American Ninja Warrior*, it is the final obstacle in each City Qualifying round and part of the City Final round. Fans of ninja warrior competitions have even created a chant—"Beat that wall!"—that they yell as athletes attempt to climb the wall. Competitors run at the wall and try to build up enough speed that they can use to launch themselves high enough to grip the upper edge of the wall and then pull themselves over the top.

Another well-known obstacle is the Jumping Spider. This obstacle consists of two parallel walls over water. Athletes take a running start and jump onto a mini trampoline to launch themselves between the two walls. They reach out with their hands and feet to grip the walls so they do not fall into the water below. Once they have secured their grip, they carefully move forward until they reach the end of the obstacle and jump down on to a mat.

The Salmon Ladder first appeared on *SASUKE*. It quickly became a favorite in ninja competitions worldwide. Competitors grab a free bar which is the bottom rung of the Salmon Ladder. While hanging from the bar, athletes propel the bar upward onto the next rungs on the ladder. The obstacle requires significant upper-body strength to move the bar up several ladder rungs. It gets its name from

DESIGNING FOR ALL WEATHER

Because ninja competitions take place outdoors, the designers must design and build obstacles that perform well and are safe in all types of weather. Athletes have competed in the extreme heat of Las Vegas and on nights when the temperature dips below freezing. Rain and moisture can cause problems with obstacles. There are many skills that cannot be tested in wet conditions. When the obstacles' surfaces are wet, competitors have a hard time keeping their balance and grip. To protect the course, the production team covers the course as soon as it starts to rain. If the rain is very light, they may add grip tape to some obstacles to make them easier to hold or for athletes to keep their footing. As soon as the weather dries up, the competition starts again.

a traditional fish ladder, which enables fish to swim past a dam by jumping up a series of steps.

One of the newer obstacles, Broken Pipes, debuted in the Kansas City qualifiers in 2017. The Broken Pipes test an athlete's balance and agility. It is made of two spinning logs and a small spring-loaded circle between them. Ninjas run across one and then the other log until they reach a landing mat. In the Kansas City Qualifiers, the Broken Pipes took out thirty-three ninjas who fell off the logs and hit the water.

CHAPTER THREE

TRAIN LIKE A NINJA

Conquering a ninja warrior obstacle course takes more than size and strength. The most successful ninjas have a mix of speed, agility, balance, upper-body strength, grip strength, and a strong core. Success on the course also requires precise timing, stamina, and explosive movements. Therefore, there is no specific ninja training regimen. Each ninja trains in her or his own way to prepare for the gauntlet of a ninja warrior course.

CLIMBING TO THE TOP

Many obstacles on a ninja warrior course involve some sort of climbing. Many

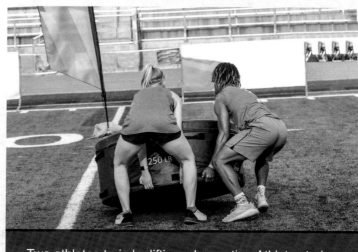

Two athletes train by lifting a heavy tire. Athletes train hard to develop the strength, endurance, and flexibility needed to succeed on a ninja warrior obstacle course.

ninjas say that adding rock climbing to their training has made them better competitors. Rock climbing requires upper-body strength, grip strength, and a strong core. Rock climbing also helps athletes learn how to swing and position their bodies and practice making on-the-spot decisions. Both skills are important when facing new obstacles that are designed to challenge and surprise athletes.

Ninja Jesse Labreck added rock climbing to her routine on the advice of other ninjas after she struggled with the Cliffhanger obstacle. Now Labreck says that rock climbing has become one of the most important parts of her training routine. She climbs three days per week, in addition to weight training, speed training, and obstacle training.

TRAINING THE HEART

Many ninjas incorporate some form of cardio work into their training. Cardio training can be running, swimming, biking, or anything that gets their muscles moving and their heart rate elevated. Cardio training strengthens the heart and lungs. This improves the athlete's endurance on the ninja course.

To improve her endurance, ninja Meagan Martin added cardio training to her workout routine. She does about an hour of cardio two to three times a week. She also climbs five to six times per week, often for three to four hours each day. She says that cardio training has been one of the most helpful elements of her ninja preparation.

GOING ON THE CIRCUIT

Circuit training can also help ninjas prepare for competition. Circuit training is a type of workout in which an athlete moves through several exercises that target different muscle groups. The athlete performs the exercises at a fast pace with little rest in between each one. A circuit training workout builds strength and muscle endurance while also providing some cardio work.

Two athletes train at the gym in a circuit training routine that targets different muscle groups while building both strength and endurance.

Ninja warrior Kevin Bull usually trains five days a week, with two easy or rest days. His workouts primarily focus on rock climbing and circuit training with weights. According to Bull, circuit training helps him build strength and endurance while also protecting his body from injury.

OBSTACLE WORK

Many ninjas include some form of obstacle work in their training. They practice on replicas of common ninja warrior obstacles like the Warped Wall or the Salmon Ladder. Kacy Catanzaro has competed on several seasons of *American Ninja Warrior*. She trains with other ninja competitors and practices on obstacles. "We love training on obstacles," she said in an interview with *Shape* magazine. "It keeps you

PRACTICE IN PARKOUR

Parkour is an extreme sport that prepares athletes for ninja warrior competitions. Parkour is the practice of navigating through obstacles in an urban or natural environment in order to get from one place to another the fastest way possible. Without using any equipment, parkour participants run, vault, jump, climb, roll, and use other movements to get from point A to point B.

The skills, strength, and agility learned in parkour translate well to ninja warrior competitions. According to *ANW* host Akbar Gbajabiamila, competitors with parkour training often go far in the competition, especially on the obstacles that test an athlete's agility.

super healthy and fit, but it's also fun. You're not dreading your workout, because it's so exciting!"

CORE STRENGTH

Having a strong core—abdominal muscles and lower back muscles—is important for ninja warrior athletes. When an athlete's core is strong, they can move their arms and legs more powerfully and with control. All athletic movements use the core in some way. Strengthening core muscles gives an athlete better balance, more body control, and more power in his or her movements.

Core strength training can take many forms. Some athletes use medicine balls and balance boards to strengthen their core muscles. Others find that rock climbing strengthens those same muscles.

MIND OVER BODY

Beyond physical fitness, ninja warriors must also be mentally tough. Each athlete has only one run to make it through the course. A slip or fall that eliminates an athlete from a competition can be extremely difficult to handle. Coming back from a devastating mistake requires a lot of mental toughness.

Ninja warrior Isaac Caldiero agrees that the mental side of being a ninja athlete is crucial for success. He does a lot of breathing exercises and positive visualization exercises to help him mentally prepare for training and competition. Kevin Bull focuses on immediate objectives and goals on the course. Doing so helps him overcome any fear or exhaustion that he experiences on the course and allows him to push himself further.

Top athletes fuel their bodies with healthy foods, such as chicken, brown rice, avocado, pepper, tomato, broccoli, red cabbage, chickpeas, lettuce, and nuts.

EAT LIKE A NINJA

What do ninja warriors eat? The answer varies by athlete. Many ninjas prefer good, clean food to fuel their bodies for better performance. They choose balanced diets with lots of protein, fruits, and vegetables to improve their stamina and strength.

Some ninjas like Isaac Caldiero prefer to eat a mostly vegetarian diet. Caldiero eats healthy and light, especially leading up to a competition. He eats very little meat and has no alcohol or caffeine.

However, other ninjas, such as Grant McCartney, admit that they do not always make the healthiest food choices. McCartney has a weakness for sweets and candy. Still, he is trying to make healthier choices because he has noticed that when he has not eaten well, his body does not respond as well to his intense training routine.

TAPER DOWN TO COMPETITION

In the months and weeks leading up to a competition, many ninjas have an intense training regimen. As the competition gets closer, however, they often taper down their workouts to be less intense. Ninja Chris Wilczewski says that tapering allows his body to recover and perform at its peak during competition. While he is tapering, Wilczewski focuses on practicing his technique on common obstacles like the Salmon Ladder or the Flying Bar.

CHAPTER FOUR

STAYING SAFE

Ninja warriors might seem like daredevils on the course. They run across spinning and wobbling logs and boards. They propel themselves off trampolines onto swings and sliders. They hang by their fingertips from obstacles high above a pit of water. As much as their stunts are extreme, these athletes and competition organizers know one thing: safety comes first.

IT STARTS WITH THE COURSE

Safety starts with the obstacle course design and construction. The crew constructs obstacles from a wood and metal skeleton. They then cover it with a layer of polyurethane followed by glossy red and silver paint.

The construction team covers every piece of exposed metal with layers of tiny cushioning. If a ninja warrior falls and hits that part of the obstacle, the cushioning will protect the athlete. The team also places thick cushioning mats all around an obstacle to protect athletes in case they fall.

The production team builds the *American Ninja Warrior* course in Cleveland, Ohio. Before the competition begins, testers will run through each obstacle to make sure it is safe.

Many obstacles are built above a 5-foot (1.5 meter) deep pool of water with a soft bottom to cushion athletes who fall.

To make sure the obstacles are safe, each one goes through extensive testing before a competition. Prototypes of obstacles are built and tested in warehouses. At each competition, the production team builds the obstacles and testers run through the course to make sure each one operates as intended on-site. If necessary, the team makes adjustments, such as changing the angle of a step or the height of an obstacle.

OVERSEERS OF SAFETY

J. J. Getskow and Spyros Vamvas are project managers who have worked on the *American Ninja Warrior* set for several seasons. They lead the teams that design, build, and manage the ninja courses in each qualifying city, along with the National Finals in Las Vegas.

Getskow and Vamvas are on set for every night of competition. Before the competition begins, they gather the production team together. "We go obstacle by obstacle by obstacle to make sure it's safe. Make sure all the padding is in place. Make sure all the clamps are tight. Make sure the obstacles are working correctly," said Vamvas in an interview posted on the American Ninja Warrior Nation

A tester jumps into an obstacle called the Frame Slider as he tests the *American Ninja Warrior* course before the filming of the show in Venice Beach, California.

website. "We're wiping down pads. We're putting towels out. Depending on the weather we might be putting tarps out to cover up, pulling them off. That's like our pre-prep before the game starts."

Once the competition starts, Getskow and Vamvas focus on making sure every athlete running the course is safe. As their team resets obstacles for the next competitor, Getskow and Vamvas follow athletes as they move through the course in case they fall or get injured. "Our ultimate goal is to watch them. In the event that they do have an injury we can clearly relay that information to the medic as he comes up. He knows he can get almost a play by play, exactly what happened to the individual. They can do their job and assess the situation," said Getskow in an interview posted on the American Ninja Warrior Nation website. On an average night of competition, the men ensure the safety of about 125 competitors.

THE RIGHT INSTRUCTIONS

Before competitors run the course, someone from the production team walks them through each obstacle. The athletes are not allowed a practice run on the obstacles. However, the team member talks to them about strategies to make it through the obstacle. The team members also tell the competitors what they are not allowed to do on each part of the course. For example, for some obstacles, athletes are not allowed to use their hands. On other obstacles, athletes may not be allowed to use their feet. The course walkthrough gives athletes an idea of what to expect during the competition, which reduces the chance of injury.

JEN HANSEN, PROFESSIONAL TESTER

In many eyes, Jen Hansen has a dream job. She works as a professional tester for the ATS Team, the company that designs and builds the obstacles for *American Ninja Warrior*. She gets paid to test and demonstrate the obstacles seen on the show. Hansen is a former college gymnast for the University of Kentucky, who won the NCAA all-around gymnastic title three times.

After noticing her work on the gymnastics-themed television show *Make It or Break It*, *American Ninja Warrior* producers asked Hansen to come test some obstacles in-house. When she made it through some obstacles, the team offered her a position working with ATS as a tester on the road as they traveled to different cities. Her favorite obstacles to test are ones that involve a trampoline. Her least favorite was the log roll.

PREVENTION IS THE BEST CURE

The training for ninja warriors is intense. To prevent injury, athletes need to make sure they do not overwork certain muscle groups and allow their bodies enough time to rest and repair. If they do not, they put themselves at risk of an injury. Ninja warrior superstar Jessie Graff says that injury prevention can be time consuming and boring, but is very important. "The biggest part that requires discipline for me is knowing when I'm supposed to rest and making sure each muscle group gets to recover as much as possible," she said in an interview posted on Refinery29.com. "I try to go to PT [physical therapy] when I have time, and I do

A woman uses a foam roller to release muscle knots and stimulate blood flow, which improves performance and speeds healing.

injury-prevention exercises … I foam roll constantly; and, I carry a lacrosse ball with me so that I can roll wherever I am because something's always sore.

At some point, every ninja warrior competitor will fall. Falls happen to everyone, from beginners to pros. By taking safety measures both on and off the course, athletes and competition organizers can make sure they are able to keep conquering many obstacles in the future.

ALL-STAR NINJAS

Many talented athletes compete on ninja warrior courses worldwide. Some have the skills to rise above the rest. These superstars on the obstacle course come from different places and backgrounds. What they all share is a passion to be the very best in their sport. Here are just a few of them.

"MIGHTY KACY"

At 5 feet (1.5 meters) tall and just under 100 pounds (45 kilograms), Kacy Catanzaro might look tiny on the course. Yet this former gymnast's drive and determination have earned her the nickname "Mighty Kacy" and made her a fan favorite. In 2014, Mighty Kacy inspired a generation of young girls when she became the first woman to conquer the 14-foot (4.3 meter) Warped Wall and the first woman to complete a city qualifying course on *American Ninja Warrior*. That same year, she also became the first woman to complete a city finals course and hit the

Kacy Catanzaro displays her muscles at the SiriusXM studios. Although she is small, Catanzaro has become a legend on the *American Ninja Warrior* course.

buzzer. Her amazing performance earned her a spot in the National Finals.

Mighty Kacy competed on ANW in 2015, 2016, and 2017 and made it to the National Finals each year. In 2016, she also competed in the original Japanese *SASUKE*. She did well, completing eight of the Stage One obstacles. At the time, she set a record, going farther than any other female athlete on the course. After the 2017 season of *American Ninja Warrior*, Catanzaro announced her retirement from the competition. Today she has moved on to wrestling with World Wrestling Entertainment (WWE).

WOLFPACK NINJA: BRIAN ARNOLD

Brian Arnold is one of *American Ninja Warrior*'s most fierce competitors. The former nursing home maintenance director first competed on the show in 2013. In his first five seasons, Arnold reached Stage Two of the National Finals in Las Vegas. In 2013, he completed Stage Two in Las Vegas and reached the Flying Bar obstacle in Stage Three, which was the farthest that any American had gone on the course at that time.

Because of his consistent success on *ANW*, Arnold was chosen in 2013 and 2014 to represent the United States in the USA vs. The World ninja warrior competition. Both times, he won his heats. Since becoming involved in ninja warrior

Ninja warrior Brian Arnold swings across an obstacle at a local ninja warrior gym. He travels around the country to encourage others to adopt a healthy lifestyle.

competitions, Arnold has left his job at the nursing home to focus on his family and training. He is part of a group of ninja warrior competitors called the Wolfpack Ninjas. Members of the Wolfpack include Arnold, "Wolfpup" Ian Dory, "Ninjadoc" Noah Kaufman, and "SheWolf" Meagan Martin. The Wolfpack Ninjas train together in Colorado and work to motivate others to pursue a healthy lifestyle.

GEOFF "POPEYE" BRITTEN

In 2014, Maryland professional cameraman Geoff Britten competed in his first *American Ninja Warrior* competition. He was quickly given the nickname of "Popeye" because of his large, muscled forearms. In his first competition season,

STRENGTH-TO-WEIGHT

In many sports, the biggest and strongest athletes are usually the most successful. That is not necessarily true for ninja warrior athletes. In this extreme sport, strength-to-weight ratio (SWR) is much more important. A SWR is calculated by the amount of weight a ninja can lift divided by the athlete's body weight. A ninja with a high SWR often performs better on the course. They can produce more power with every action, allowing them to run and jump faster. They perform better in suspension obstacles that feature rings or bars. While adding muscle can improve an athlete's strength, too much excess muscle can lower an athlete's SWR. A heavier, more muscled body means the athlete will have to expend more energy to carry their weight throughout the course. To improve SWR, athletes often perform bodyweight exercises such as pushups, pullups, and core work.

Britten made it to the National Finals, but was eliminated in Stage One on the Jumping Spider obstacle.

The following year, Britten again advanced to the National Finals. This time, he amazed fellow athletes and fans by becoming the first competitor to finish all four stages of the National Finals. However, his moment of glory was cut short when competitor Isaac Caldiero also finished the National Finals and scaled the fourth stage of Mount Midoriyama a few minutes later. Because Caldiero's time was seconds faster than Britten's time, Caldiero won the $1 million prize and the title of American Ninja Warrior.

Along the way to the top of Mount Midoriyama, Britten completed all six obstacle courses from the city qualifying rounds to the four stages of the National Finals and hit the buzzer at the end of each one for a perfect season. To date, Britten is the only ninja warrior athlete to have completed a perfect season.

SUPERWOMAN JESSIE GRAFF

Professional stuntwoman Jessie Graff is one of the most popular and well-known athletes on American Ninja Warrior. In her rookie season in 2013, she became the first woman to qualify for a City Finals. Although she did not finish the City Finals course, she earned a wild card selection and became one of two women to reach the Jumping Spider at the National Finals.

In 2015, Graff earned a spot in the National Finals, becoming only the second woman after Kacy Catanzaro to qualify for the Las Vegas competition. In 2016, she again earned a spot at the National Finals and became the first woman to get up the Warped Wall in Stage One. She also made history as the first woman to complete Stage One in the Las Vegas finals. In 2017, Graff again qualified for the National Finals, but fell on the Flying Squirrel before she could finish Stage One.

In 2017, Graff was chosen to become the first woman to compete for Team USA in the USA vs. the World ninja warrior competition. In the competition, three teams—USA, Europe, and Latin America—competed in three heats on each stage of the Las Vegas finals course. Graff joined other USA ninjas Jake Murray, Josh Levin, Daniel Gil, Drew Drechsel, and Brian Arnold. In the contest, Graff set another

Jessie Graff leaps in the air on the red carpet before a screening event for *American Ninja Warrior* at Universal Studios Hollywood in 2016.

record and became the first woman ever to finish Stage Two of the course. Team USA took first place in the competition.

ISAAC CALDIERO

Isaac Caldiero, a former busboy and professional climber, had always been a big fan of Japan's ninja warrior competition *SASUKE*. When he learned that a version of the competition was coming to the United States, he was immediately interested in trying it. After talking to a friend who had competed on the show, Caldiero created a submission video for the show's casting agency. His video featured his life and skills as a professional climber and his hobbies of juggling and biking. Even so, producers did not pick him to compete. Instead, he had to wait for his chance in the walk-on line.

His patience paid off, and in 2013 Caldiero was one of the walk-ons that made it into the competition. He wanted to stand out from the other competitors, so he walked to the starting line in a leftover Jesus costume from Halloween. His performance was even more memorable. His first year, Caldiero made it all the way to the National Finals in Las Vegas, where he was knocked out on the Jumping Spider obstacle. The next year, he made it to Stage Two of the National Finals before falling on the Salmon Ladder.

Caldiero was determined to go even farther on the course. He trained relentlessly, seven days a week, on a homemade course in his parents' backyard. The training paid off in 2015, when Caldiero completed all four stages of the National Finals. Although fellow ninja Geoff Britten ran the course first and completed it, Caldiero finished with a faster time and was crowned the winner of American Ninja Warrior and the $1 million prize.

Caldiero believes that the mental toughness that he developed over his years of free-solo climbing, without ropes and harnesses, gives him an edge in ninja warrior competitions. "I do a lot of free-solo type climbing where my life is literally in my own hands. At times, falling is not an option, and I can't let my nerves get to me. Otherwise I die, and I don't want to die," Caldiero said in an interview posted on the *Houston Chronicle* website. "So I took that same mentality into this course. Not only was there this impossible feat that was driving me to accomplish, but in the back of my mind, I said I couldn't fall."

EXTREME COURSES, EXTREME THRILLS

Ninja warrior competitions are a thrilling sport for people around the world. Each ninja obstacle course presents new and exciting challenges for athletes to conquer. For athletes and fans around the world, this extreme sport provides extreme entertainment and thrills.

GLOSSARY

agility The ability to move quickly and easily.

brainstorm A group discussion meant to create and talk about new ideas.

cardio training Exercises that get the heart pumping and lungs working.

endurance Being able to do something or perform for a long period of time.

gauntlet An intimidating series of challenges.

grip strength The force applied by the hands to pull on or suspend from an object.

ninja Anyone who is adept at a particular skill or ability.

obstacle A challenge that a ninja warrior must go through or over in order to move forward on the course.

passion A strong enthusiasm for something.

prototype A preliminary model of something.

rookie Someone who is new to an event or competition.

rungs The horizontal supports on a ladder.

stage A section of a course.

stamina The ability to sustain physical activity.

taper To gradually lessen.

urban A city environment.

visualization To form a mental picture of something.

FOR MORE INFORMATION

American Ninja Warrior
NBC Universal
30 Rockefeller Plaza
New York, NY 10112
Website: www.nbc.com/american-ninja-warrior
Facebook, Instagram, and Twitter: @ninjawarrior
This is the official website for the television competition
   show *American Ninja Warrior*. The site offers information
   about the latest seasons, episodes on demand, casting
   information, and other news.

Athlete Warrior Games
Email: awg@athletewarriorgames.com
Website: www.athletewarriorgames.com
Facebook: @athletewarriorgames
Athlete Warrior Games sponsors a series of ninja
   competitions at gyms across the country. It uses a
   scoring system that includes speed and also factors
   in the methods used by competitors to overcome
   each obstacle.

Canadian Ninja League
77 Edmonton Trail NE
Calgary, AB T2E 8M8
Canada
Website: http://cnl.ninja
Facebook and Instagram: @canadianninjaleague
The Canadian Ninja League is Canada's first and only
   competitive ninja warrior league in Canada. Its goal is to
   be the central organization for all Ninja Warrior news and
   information about training and competitions.

Climbing Escalade Club (CEC)
Email: cec.ed@climbingcanada.ca
Website: http://climbingcanada.ca/en/home
Facebook and Twitter: @climbingcanada
The CEC is a national sport organization created to
    regulate and promote competition climbing in Canada, a
    discipline similar to ninja warrior skills.

National Ninja League
Email: info@nationalninja.com
Website: www.nationalninja.com
Facebook: @nationalninjaleague
The National Ninja League is a nonprofit organization
    formed by several of the country's top ninja facilities to
    promote the sport of ninja obstacle courses across the
    United States.

Ultimate Ninja Athlete Association (UNAA)
(505) 980-0149
Website: www.ultimateninja.net
Facebook: @ultimateninjaathlete
Twitter: @ultimateninjaa1
The UNAA is a global organization that organizes a series
    of ninja obstacle course competitions at gyms around
    the world.

Butler, Erin K. *Extreme Land Sports*. North Mankato, MN: Capstone Press, 2018.

Frisch-Schmoll, Joy. *Rock Climbing*. Mankato, MN: Creative Education, 2018.

Gitlin, Marty. *Extreme Sports and their Greatest Competitors*. New York, NY: Britannica Educational Publishing, 2015.

Hapka, Cathy. *Junior Ninja Champion: The Competition Begins*. New York, NY: Houghton Mifflin Harcourt, 2018.

Hapka, Cathy. *Junior Ninja Champion: The Fastest Finish*. New York, NY: Houghton Mifflin Harcourt, 2019.

Jackson, Demi. *Parkour*. New York, NY: Gareth Stevens Publishing, 2016.

Loh-Hagan, Virginia. *Extreme Parkour*. Ann Arbor, MI: Cherry Lake Publishing, 2016.

Loh-Hagan, Virginia. *Extreme Rock Climbing*. Ann Arbor, MI: Cherry Lake Publishing, 2016.

NBC Entertainment. *Become an American Ninja Warrior: The Ultimate Insider's Guide*. New York, NY: St. Martin's Griffin, 2018.

Shea, Therese. *Rock and Ice Climbing*. New York, NY: Rosen Publishing, 2016.

BIBLIOGRAPHY

Angle, Sara. "The Mighty Kacy Catanzaro Is Ready for Round Three." Shape.com, June 5, 2015. http://www.shape.com/celebrities/interviews/mighty-kacy-catanzaro-ready-round-three.

Bleiberg, Larry. "10 Gyms Where You Can Try a 'Ninja Warrior' Course." *USA Today*, January 11, 2019. http://www.usatoday.com/story/travel/destinations/10greatplaces/2019/01/11/ninja-warrior-gyms-where-try-popular-obstacle-courses/2497290002.

Bradley, Ryan. "Behind the Scenes of 'American Ninja Warrior'." Outside Online.com, May 21, 2015. http://www.outsideonline.com/1981091/behind-scenes-american-ninja-warrior.

Cespedes, Andrea. "Ideal Strength-to-Weight Ratio." Livestrong.com. Retrieved March 31, 2019. http://www.livestrong.com/article/461397-ideal-weight-to-strength-ratio.

Goldberg, Lesley. "'American Ninja Warrior' Crowns First Winner—With a Twist." *Hollywood Reporter*, September 14, 2015. http://www.hollywoodreporter.com/live-feed/american-ninja-warrior-winner-isaac-822411.

Lee, Nikki. "Behind the Scenes Where the American Ninja Warrior Obstacles Are Born." American Ninja Warrior Nation, October 5, 2016. http://www.americanninjawarriornation.com/2016/10/5/13164268/american-ninja-warrior-obstacles-are-made-ats-production-shop.

Lee, Nikki. "Jen Hansen Has the Coolest Job on American Ninja Warrior." American Ninja Warrior Nation, August 17, 2016. http://www.americanninjawarriornation.com/2016/8/17/12505826/jen-hansen-has-the-coolest-job-on-american-ninja-warrior.

Lee, Nikki. "Meet the Green Hats, the People in Charge of the American Ninja Warrior Course." American Ninja Warrior Nation, October 5, 2016. https://www .americanninjawarriornation.com/2016/10/5/13165084/green -hats-people-in-charge-of-the-american-ninja-warrior-course -spyros-vamvas-jj-getskow

Loh-Hagan, Virginia. *Extreme Parkour*. Ann Arbor, MI: Cherry Lake Publishing, 2016.

Maness, Tracy. "Only 'American Ninja Warrior' Winner Teaches Clinics at Heights Rock Gym." *Houston Chronicle*, March 12, 2018. https://www.chron.com/neighborhood/heights/news /article/Only-American-Ninja-Warrior-winner-teaches -12746765.php

Obstacle Academy. Retrieved March 25, 2019. https://www .obstacle-academy.com/our-story.

Prudom, Laura. "American Ninja Warrior Crowns First Ever Winner After 7 Seasons." Variety.com, September 14, 2015. https://variety.com/2015/tv/news/american-ninja-warrior -winner-isaac-caldiero-geoff-britten-season-7 -finale-1201593633.

Siler, Wes. "How Ninja Warrior Jessie Graff Became a Real-Life Superhero," OutsideOnline.com, October 28, 2016. http:// www.outsideonline.com/2130936/how-ninja-warrior-jessie -graff-became-real-life-superhero.

Stieg, Cory. "How These Real Women Train For American Ninja Warrior." Refinery29.com, August 31, 2017. http://www .refinery29.com/en-us/2017/08/170118/how-to-train-for -american-ninja-warrior-women#slide-2.

Ultimate Ninja Athlete Association. Retrieved March 25, 2019. https://www.ultimateninja.net/about.

INDEX

ABOUT THE AUTHOR

Carla Mooney is a graduate of the University of Pennsylvania. Today, she writes for young people and is the author of many books for young adults and children. Mooney enjoys learning about new sports and leisure activities. She is an avid fan of *American Ninja Warrior* and attended the City Qualifying round held at the Carrie Furnace in Pittsburgh, Pennsylvania.

PHOTO CREDITS